A BEGINNER'S GUIDE TO CHEATING

A Beginner's Guide To Cheating

Poems

ANDY JACKSON

RED SQUIRREL PRESS

First published in the UK in 2015 by Red Squirrel Press
www.redsquirrelpress.com

Red Squirrel Press is distributed by Central Books Ltd. and
represented by Inpress Ltd.
www.inpressbooks.co.uk

Designed and typeset by Gerry Cambridge
www.gerrycambridge.com

A CIP catalogue record is available from the British Library.

ISBN: 978 1910437 11 7

Printed in the UK by Martin the Printers Ltd. on acid-free paper
sourced from mills with the FSC chain of custody certification.
www.martins-the-printers.com

For Evie and Catriona

Contents

Caution

You do not have to say anything
but it may harm your defence
if you do not mention, when questioned,
something which you later rely on
in court. Anything you do say
may be given in evidence.
Do you understand?

You do not have to answer anything.
If you understand the harm
of what you say, do not rely on courts
or evidence to defend you later.
When questioned, do not mention
anything, do not say anything.
Do you understand?

Question anything you do not understand,
but do not court their questions.
Understand that they do not
rely on evidence for their defence.
Anything that harms them
can also be used against you.
Do you understand?

You have the right to remain silent
and, when there is only silence,
you will remain.

A Beginner's Guide To Cheating

Beware your first deception. It is elegant
by nature and will write itself on everything
you touch, a retrovirus you cannot erase.

Learn to meet the gaze of strangers;
eliminate the facial tics and quirks
that better men can read like prose.

Practice sleight of hand, stolen ace
up one sleeve, blackjack up the other;
both play out the same way in the end.

Intercept the ballot papers; grease
the palms of independent monitors,
sleep with whomsoever is required.

Treat all opportunities as friends,
all friends as property, all property
as evidence. Burn what can't be carried.

Load the dice and rig the wheel,
stack the deck and check the exits.
Is the car outside, its engine running?

Avoid all substances that amplify
performance (see *Appendix 1*); what
you don't absorb cannot be traced.

Do not offer ignorance as proof of
innocence; only fools believe
that fools can be believed.

If challenged, do not swear on graves
of mothers, eyes or lives of children;
such oaths reveal you like a flare.

Before you start, remember: if they catch
you out, they might as well have caught you
going through the pockets of the dead.

Appendix One : *Substances deemed to enhance performance illegally*

Human Growth Hormone, Nandrolone, Atenolol, Erythropoietin,
Ephedrine, Dexedrine, Ovaltine, Lucozade, White Wine Spritzers,
Tequila Slammers, Newton & Ridley's, Ben & Jerry's, Chanel No.5,
Jackson Pollock's No.19, Wilson Pickett's 'Land of 1000 Dances', the
feet of Uma Thurman, the smile on Robert De Niro's face at the end
of *Once Upon A Time In America,* the confidence of Bruce Forsyth
and any otherwise unaccountable manifestation of *joie de vivre.*

Dactylography

I looked for you in what was left behind;
The programmes that you Sky-plussed,
the recipes that only worked for you

though I assiduously followed every line.
I hoped to find you, latent in the dust,
so swept each surface for a residue,

resorting to my fingerprinting kit,
its stock of powder, magnifying glass,
the little book to keep my findings in.

I thought I might find evidence to fit
my theories, chance impressions, lost
among the corrugations of your skin,

but in looking for a pattern in the stripes
I missed the lonely speck of blood,
the pillow with its single strand of hair,

the glass you drank from, partly wiped
of prints, the version of events that said
how you were not there, there, not there.

Crossroads

You used to take your Rickenbacker on the plane,
booked an extra seat for it. You didn't trust
the baggage crews. It once belonged to Weller,
long ago—heads you keep it, tails it goes on eBay.

Rotterdam, late afternoon, late summer. Blues.
You never really got The Blues. The sound of tuning up
across the park, a squall of feedback, humid air, the sky
sucks up the chords. A Robert Johnson cover sung in Dutch.

This is a sign. You traded your soul, but then forgot
the value of your shares may fall as well as rise.
The Devil has been round. He wants his due, but will
consolidate your loans in one affordable damnation.

You wonder why it never felt like this before, why chord
progressions never rang so clear, and then
you realise the ringing is the quarter hour, a chime
from belfry tiled in hellish red. It's true. He has you every time.

The Academie Française Considers A Word For 'Dogging'

Chiennage, a literal response, is cast aside,
its laziness the thin end of the wedge, reminder
that the Anglophones are twenty miles across
the ruffled sleeve of water, typing into *blogues*

and laughing in their pockets at *le yé-yé*, snide
and covetous and lacking in *élan*. They ponder
whether poetry would work, consider coarse
equivalents—*attroupement de rut*, though stags

are cheapened by comparison with sleazy
rosbifs blundering priapically in leisurewear.
Dehorgie is a possibility, a cut-and-shut creation
with a pleasing wit. *Etranger-plonger*—smirks

from younger duffers round the room—easy
on the ear but too contrived. Onomatopoeia
puts its hand up after momentary hesitation,
volunteers *ouambam*. Chairman says it doesn't work

for him, and *dingue-dongue, shique-shaque, fouhaha*
make shagging in a layby sound okay.
Someone mentions gender—*masculin ou feminin?*—
and that's enough to force adjournment for the day.

Zelocracy

They emerged, a flashmob from the shadows,
growing in number every time our backs
were turned. They lost their accents, learned
Estuarine, upskilled. Now they hide in plain sight,
gatekeepers for nonformation and antifacts,
contriving fallacies like sausages, blamestorming
on twitter streams, duking it out with liberals,
wearing their avatars like chainmail, holding forth
on middle-class moralysis, how the past
is the new future. Welcome to the Darwikian age;
government by crowd-sourcing, the bloc
that can't be stopped, genned up and ready to rock.

Immortality Now!

My passing was reported on the midday news,
not entirely unexpected, to be truthful. I'd been ill
for years—a vague malaise, a slow decline, the booze
and fags anaesthetising what they could not kill.

The label plans to re-release my greatest hits,
with lavish packaging and honeyed liner notes
from Quincy Jones. I'd expect no less than this.
The correspondents google up some quotes

from former friends whose tweets record
their eulogies. My third wife may curate
a screening of my early work, available to download,
and then a comprehensive retrospective at the Tate.

I'm told a choir of looms is standing by in West Bengal
to hum fortissimo with swathes of bombazine
for dresses for the hundred thousand girls
who now observe the proper forms, while magazines

go public with their baseless claims of infidelity,
parade the kids with eyes that could be mine.
The *Daily Mail* reads homosexuality
in letters to a college friend in nineteen eighty-nine.

The biopic is slated for a spring release; I'm played
by some Australian, I'm sure an unintended slight.
Too much, perhaps, to hope for light and shade,
but you would think he'd get my accent right.

They crowded in on me towards the end, to see
the credits roll and hear the national anthem play.
The more they reminisced about the real me
the more dead I became. Before I slipped away

I thought of Grandad's brother Joe, his modest span
complete before my birth, his passing hardly a loss,
and yet I carried something of his worth, the last man
to remember the last man to remember who he was.

Tent Revival in Ozone Park

'There's just no two ways about it. The Dostioffskis, the cops, the
Lee Anns, all the evil skulls of this world, are out for our skin. It's
up to us to see that nobody pulls any schemes on us. They've got a
lot more up their sleeves beside a dirty arm. Remember that. You
can't teach the old maestro a new tune.'
—Jack Kerouac, On The Road

They pulled some schemes on us, yes,
but here we are, inheritors of the kingdom,
writing our own catechisms, suitcase full
of marital aids, blank notebooks, old 78s.

There's tunes out there for all us, I guess,
blacktop ballads and diner dirges. Sing 'em
and you're tuned to angels, bum notes and all,
hang around for your cue and it's a long wait.

Treat every day like it's the last, and head west
if you like your oranges ripe. Keep your income
close to your outgoings, enter any shortfall
in the ledgers. Pay your taxes to the state.

We're always dogged by unbelievers, but flesh
is just a vestment of the soul, and not the sum
of what we are. Are you willing to testify? Call
His name, raise your hand. *Amen.* It ain't too late.

Analogue

I am older than you think,
having lived through years
of hearing my own voice
on cheap cassettes, deformed
by episodes of wow and flutter,
heads in misalignment, until
my eventual unspooling.

I have run my fingers round
a vinyl rim, a spiral scratch
rotating on the spindle of your eye.
I've listened without hearing,
absorbing the distractions
of each pop and crackle, until
all that's left is imperfection.

Lately we've stopped looking
for a pristine copy of ourselves,
remastered without overdubs,
but after all these years,
at least we're listening again
for the full-frequency experience,
the sounds beneath the sounds.

A Poem Is Coming For You

A poem is coming for you, an old car,
walnut dashboard, leather trim, driven
by a person you have never met, who
seems to know the way, the short cuts
and the minor roads. They warn you
that they cannot guarantee to take you
where you want to go, and that
the brakes could fail at any moment.

The poem could be someone you have seen,
maybe in the street. You pass them daily,
though you don't acknowledge them.
Once, you heard them whistling a tune
you thought you knew, a childhood song,
a lung full of smoke; their dark cloak
parted, flashed a hint of iridescent lining
in a colour even poets could not name.

Sometimes the poem is an animal. It knows
to stay downwind of you, out of sight.
You heard it nosing round your bins
last night, looking for the things you tried
to throw away. It doesn't care about you;
you are just another creature, scared
and hungry, but it's smart, and one day
it will find out how to get into your home.

Drive-Thru

Not for me the hands soft as hammers,
inspecting every stonechip, door-scuff,
micro-dent. No wringing out of chamois,
scowling at the clouds, gulls. A man's love

is not enough; the roads must all be clear
and free of the corroding breath of salt.
Across the way a youth in outdoor gear
powers up his jetwash, earnest to a fault,

oblivious to weather or its words of caution,
telling him that paths are never free from dust,
and how he'll labour through each season,
sanding, priming, touching-up the creeping rust.

He'll hump his pail of asses' milk from tap
to path to driveway, soap down crevices
and fairings, watch sill-gathered juices drip
on asphalt, draining to the street like promises

of irrigation in an arid land. I still dream
of drive-thrus, the roaring rollers, smiling
Slavs who bustle with brushes, while streams
of triplewax give way to hot air, peeling

back my wrinkled skin. This is the tunnel
of love, or as close as I will get; shapes
in darkness, noise, latent terror, till the final
nudging out, the notice saying *please try your brakes.*

Cargo Cult

Long before the rasping of the anchor
or the clang of hull on dock

you hear the tempo of the harbour,
the groan of crane and truck

and scrape of hobnail boot. It's night,
a blind-eye-turning darkness, hotter

than a skillet, summer at its height.
You've plodded half a world of water,

hold full of lumber and a crate
of premonitions from Barrett Strong

and Howlin' Wolf, worth their weight
in benzedrine. It won't be long

till white wraiths appear, ragged wads
of cash passing hand to hand

like plague, haggling for the goods
no shop will stock. The bands

without a name will gorge on riffs
and basslines, puzzle over chords

and fingering, the tricky fifths
and augmentations, learning words

that they would never use in school
and fighting over who can bleed

the blues. The alchemy begins; scales
undress, the rhythms interbreed,

shanties that they learned as kids
insinuate themselves in harmony

and rhyme; impenetrable codes
are broken with each change of key.

They'll go from village hall to Savile Row
in less time than it takes to raise

a fire; the opening number of the show
an overture for the closing of the age.

Camp Freddy's Lament

We haven't talked like this for years—was it '68?
Those frantic minutes on the mountainside,
the world see-sawing, undecided. The weight
was always shifting, but a cataclysmic slide
was coming, in Paris or some other failed state.

The optimist in all of us was so preoccupied
with endings that we never thought to look
at how the Fifties changed the rules. Besides,
the public never had the time to read the book
and therefore only had the movies as a guide,

where their idea of a heist was Holloway
and Guinness with their phoney Eiffel Towers.
Ambitious, yes, but trust the script to underplay
the menace, not a gun in sight for two hours,
possibly the reason why they almost got away

with it. We took that London charm to heart,
where villains did the right thing by their mums,
but soon we learned you had to look the part,
Anderson & Sheppard suits, king of the slums
but still not knowing *a la mode* from *a la carte*.

So, if you want to know what happened next,
if the promise of a great idea came and went,
all I can reveal is what you probably expect—
we never really worked it out, and this lament
was bagged along with all my personal effects.

In the absence of a sequel, or a post-credit reveal
I can tell you; there never was a driver at the wheel.

Dignity

after Sean O'Brien

Give me a pear from the blue bowl, Jane.
Give me five a day, for old time's sake.
Peel me a grape, disembowel a fig.
Let fruit be waiting when I wake.

Pour me a glass of the finest, Jane.
Wine with the strength to dismember the speech
We need them to know our intemperance.
A glass of Ribena. Sex On The Beach.

Play me a song from your canon, Jane.
Strum like you strummed on our days on the loose.
Sing of the world we found no way to live in,
songs of the shotgun, the razor, the noose.

Write down the words we agreed on, Jane.
Remember, they'll look for the flaws in your hand,
so keep it compact, don't sketch in the margin,
and never give reasons. They won't understand.

Hold onto my hand. It is time, Jane.
Set down your drink. It will never grow cold.
Our eyes may stay open. Our lungs may not rattle.
No closing music. No credits to roll.

Give me a pear from the blue bowl, Jane.
Give me five a day, for old time's sake.
Peel me a grape, disembowel a fig.
Let someone be waiting when we awake.

In Other News

Waiter in the cool bodega has a party piece;
at dinner's end he whips the tablecloth away
with single wrist-snap, leaves a bare table,
cutlery and plates unmoved, smiling as he
flourishes the cloth before him like a matador.

Behind him is a live feed on the television;
correspondents lined against familiar walls
speaking into cameras all down a street,
saying how this humdrum town may never
come to terms with it, may never be the same.

Next day we will look for photos in the
foreign press, rummage through the channels
for a fragment of the British news, noting
how it's getting darker earlier back home,
shadows lengthened by a sun that tilts away.

The waiter clears another table. Imagine
all those nights of practice with the chipped
and broken pots, rehearsing every move,
believing he could pull it off, do the deed,
yet leave the fragile things untouched.

Allogeneic

I know the substance they have drawn
from me. I've felt it drip from razor-nicks
into the sink, put bloodied finger to my lips
and learned the taste of what I am,
bitter as walnuts and thinner than spit.

I lie awake and feel the clots, strung out
like threaded beads, bumping through
my veins, then dream of you, my sibling,
out there somewhere, twinned by crossmatch,
topping up your tanks with liquid me.

Take, then, the blood of my blood, typed
against type, all that I can spare and stay alive.
Beware the strange contagion of its brew,
and should a new affliction rise unheralded,
bubbling like Moët through your carotid,

it could be me, surprising you like hiccups
in the night, a sudden myoclonus that taps
my name in morse upon your diaphragm,
a benign infection, a voice you can't place,
a cough or a thought you cannot shake.

Fàgail

He is the last of all to leave this place,
waiting for the Admiralty sloop, a refugee
pursued by no-one. Hands like claws
and scabrous skin the pallor of the sea,
he wears the North Atlantic on his face.

His home is ceded to the slew of gulls,
immutable chaos of beak and feather,
the only real government here. The fall
of man approaches, low pressure
roaring in, a revolutionary squall.

Throughout inconstancies of weather
he has clung like topsoil to the fact
of this isle, but, as would a doomed lover,
it now pushes him away, a wordless act
of kindness, knowing it is over.

The final parliament dissolved, the vote
not carried, it is time to face the sea
again and set adrift the seaborne note
that says that you were here, that we
were here. Now, step onto the boat.

Long Haul

I worry that one day we'll leave our bags
unguarded for too long. Security with dogs
will sniff around them, come to the decision
to destroy them in controlled explosions.
We sometimes walk away and don't attend
to what we lug between us. Crunching sand
in shoes annoys like missing buttons on a shirt,
reminders of the things which, at the start,
we planned to reconstruct together
but now are happy to forgive of one another.

We know that, for as long as we have flown together,
a change of weather changes more than weather.
We exchange our boarding cards for empty air
which isn't nothing, simply nothing to declare.

Listening Post

In the name of national security
she listens in and scans the secret hours
for emblems of sedition in the fifth estate,

some fresh intelligence. Obscurity
bestows upon her fascinating powers,
although the suppositions that she makes

are not her own but drawn from lists
—transactions for a hundredweight
of weed-killer, twilight Google search

for Sarin, twenty texts from anarchist
to his cabal, some random future dates.
Outside the cable nexus, she could purge

herself of training, take the weekend drugs
and be with him tonight. The faintest click,
the line connects. A dial tone, the tap is set.

She hears him phone out from the snug,
some pub in rain-dipped northern bailiwick,
imagines him sat there. In silhouette

he is the very devil, cosy with Bakunin,
dressed in Lyle & Scott. The idle dream
begins—she says his name as they rush up to bed,

they talk of getting out somehow. The tuning
fades, but someone's watching her on-screen.
Her mobile rings. *Click.* The line goes dead.

Hey Presto

'Any sufficiently advanced technology is indistinguishable
from magic.'
                                            —Arthur C. Clarke

We've been getting high on heavy water,
wiping lipstick from the Erlenmeyer flask,
passing it around, looking for some order
in the chaos of flavours, oblivious to risk

or scientific rigour. We joined The Craft
at twenty-two, imagined it a closed society;
hard to join, impossible to leave, the last
of the charlatans, or the new technocracy.

A dozen generations back they might
have burned us at the stake for this;
drawing fire from dumb stones or life
from wasted organs, making light from gas,

but now the mob has left us all to play
with any toy we can afford, from petri
dish to cyclotron, trusting us to slay
all pathogens, liquidate each deadly

vector while it sleeps, make advances
to the particles that lurk in theories.
Let us read your palm; the chances
are you'll live forever. Two *Hail Marys*,

two *Our Fathers*, tablets to be taken
after meals. Mix the elements, then stand
for thirty minutes; two parts speculation,
one part luck. Say the magic words, and...

Lines On A Royal Wedding

Do you take this woman?
Do you take her to have and to hold
but particularly to have, repeatedly,
on the horse-hair stuffing
of the bed of your ancestors
while the footman waits, discreetly,
till you're spent, then steps in
to remove the royal prophylactic?

Do you promise to love this woman,
love and honour her? Not the
constitutional imperatives of love,
but the eyes-rolled-back abandon
of the union, the fizz of lust
that bursts as she divests herself
of ermine-trimmed bikini
and whispers in your ear *Your...Majesty.*

Do you promise to obey?
Obey the things which no-one
should ignore—the glory of the orb
and sceptre, weighed in trembling hands,
shyly in the shadowed light, then curious,
then unashamed and commonplace,
a part of what you are, inevitable
as the changing of the guard.

Radioactivity

In the store behind the classroom I received
a first consensual exposure, a coin of Americium,
barely found in nature, exquisitely decaying,
a thimbleful of millirads, *get it while it's hot*. Nested

like a medal in its felt-lined box, I believed
its voice of energy conferred with me alone, numb,
approaching critical mass. I still hear it, saying
this is the half-life you have lived, and wasted.

I Am The Clock That Winds The Doomed Man

sure that you, like me, lament the passive trust
in ingenuity which blunts the days that remain.
My role has only ever been to nudge the crust
you float your cities on, or lace the rain
with what you leak into the sky. Do not test
impartial glaciers, or think the seas benign,
when surely you must know even the best
can only swim so long with bellies full of brine.
Something in your optimism would suggest
a mastery of fate, the skill to lower waterlines
or kill the heat; extrapolations say you're dead as dust.

Surely you must long for endless snows, the air
a counterweight to sea, the land free of the plough,
the seaborne cows we took for mermaids or the roar
of mammoths in the tundra. You need somehow
to set aside these minor-scale extinctions and inure
yourself to this; that you were fractionated long ago,
distilled from hydrocarbons at your crude core,
and when compressed and stratified below
the sediments that mass upon you, what endures
will be prospected and extracted over time, to flow
through pumps to drive new industry, somewhere
among the sundry futures that await you now.

The Ladies of B-Wing Topless Calendar

Miss January (infant strangler)
loves Madonna, Chinese food and shoes,
talked around to posing for the camera—
that arse, those legs—nice stocking fillers,
if you get my drift. You'd hardly know
the things she's done, her skin so smooth,
her tan lines fading into tide marks.
Bikini straps hang down like limp spaghetti,
eyes not blank and sullen like a killer
but shining with the power of her body.

Miss June (the Preston Poisoner)
likes Ronan Keating, keeps Alsatians,
puckers up and looks at the photographer,
perhaps at me, or maybe at herself,
imagining the jolting rounds of hand relief.
Great idea, something for the lads
while pulling in the fivers for a charity,
cheques pinned to death threats in the mail.
Her grand concealments, all her simple plans
which could not fail, refracted by the lens.

We need to see more. Would you move your hands away?
We've been a bad, bad boy. Now, you must pay.

Dead Letter Drop

I agree to pass some poems on to him, each
one as predictable as closing time.
I write them up; he writes them off, his speech
and mannerisms populating every line.

What he leaves for me is contraband;
incriminating signatures, yellowing photographs,
an envelope of observations in a hand
so shaky that they might as well be hieroglyphs.

He leaves them in the place we agreed, out of sight;
takes the long way home, slips into the lake of night.

Immorality Now

I am heir-apparent to a graceless dynasty,
building my portfolio in landmines, driving
up the price of grain in fourth-world nations,
asset-stripping, selling futures. Trade is thriving.

I've not been clean since sixteen, but the vices
of the past can now be treated as diseases.
It's great to be straight, but spritzing water
into Bolly was the neatest trick that Jesus

ever turned. Did I tell you how I had my way
with mother, daughter and precocious cousin,
all of them within a week, none of them aware
that I had bagged the set? There are dozens

of them out there if you know the places
where they go. Once they sniff the stench
of middle age they're panic-buying petrol
for the fires their husbands cannot quench.

I take day-trips to Norfolk, gassing badgers,
sleeping with the locals, spitting in their cider.
In my dreams I'm crouching in a jungle hide,
gun in hand, waiting for the last white tiger.

Today I came across a tiny wounded bird,
wings disjointed, heart ballooning in the wreck
of feathers. I smoothed them down, looked
into its trusting eye, and wrung its neck.

Girl From The Polders

In her youth she worked and drank
and danced on artificial islands, lying low
on concrete piles, a gag in the throat
of a gulping estuary. Living with
the prospect of Atlantean collapse
into the shallows turned her on,
made each day a mortal dare. From then
she always lived on reclaimed ground,
on floating fens and marshes, or a year
on Black Sea salt-pans where the waters
turned to heavy air. She settled down
behind the dykes and tidal booms
of Europe, thrilled by threat of flood
each year as oceans stared her out.
She was deaf to claims that she'd be safe
on mountains or in landlocked fields.
She knew the plates were always shifting,
while she slept the continents made fire together.

Her men were all poor swimmers, in too deep,
rescued from maternal homes, some pulled
from sodden benches in the park, or met in rain
at prison gates. She gave them mouth-to-mouth
and wrang them out, taught them strokes she knew,
then lead them out beyond the danger flags
to where she had dominion over tides.
She had faith in anything that she could build,
mistrusting the chicaneries of nature,
excited by the thought her men could leave
at any time, return to priggish mothers,
hit the welcome bottle, maybe kill again.

She knows enough of tides to turn her back
on them, embrace the shallow breathing
of the sea. She sits in darkness, in control,
monitoring rates of flow and regulating sluices,
lowering the barrage, holding back the flood.

Market Forces Sweetheart

What kind of town is this? Nowhere to chain the bike,
railings full as inquisitionary racks, train strike
in its twenty-seventh day, talks suspended.
You were solid once, but poison in the papers
has a hold, comradeship reduced to vapour
in the elemental fires of the capital. Safer
to rely on debit cards than cash, or human nature.
Your Visa card sees all—which credit is extended,
which peccadilloes cannot be excused. You touch
its corners in your pocket. Flexible, but not that much.

What you really need, apart from futons and a toaster,
is a sense of life lived in the black. The glossy posters
talk of easy terms, economies beyond comprehension.
God knows you could use a little slack,
a payment holiday. Perhaps a measured shock,
a busted boom, a closing of the books,
might end the never-never. It's five o'clock
here in the pantheon, the tannoy barks attention.
We take our shoes and socks off, join the crowds above,
sing the corporate anthem in the shopping mall of love.

Northern Rock

Another year without a summer,
gone like that. Wise to carry an umbrella
in a place like this, perhaps for rain,
though who knows what might fall today?

Night struggles with its overcoat,
as bone-grey office blocks put out
lights and draw the shutters down.
A florist says she's never known

it be like this, as she arranges
white chrysanthemums. Front page
of the *Evening News* talks of mayhem
on the trading floor, the endgame

playing out inexorably for us all.
A spring's reported in the east, the fall
of autocrats, their looted riches gone
to Grand Cayman or the Isle of Man.

Tomorrow there'll be queues outside
the bank again, but at least tonight
I'll sleep, my mattress stuffed with fivers,
one day older, not much wiser.

Resettlement

Here's the deal. They've got it in for you.
They haven't got your number, but
they're working on it, talking to your dad.
Photoshopped you ten years older,

bulked you up, added jowls and creases.
If he's still alive, this might be how he'd look.
No good lying doggo in the long grass
when they specialise in slash and burn.

As each new moral panic settles in
you wonder if you've been forgotten,
dropped into a well without a wish?
No, there are files that never close,

grudges ground on whetstones year-on-year,
bearers waiting for their moment
in a room alone with you. Mothers, sisters,
who surprise themselves with anger,

planning for their picnic by the gallows.
So don't come over all surprised, and don't
imagine I'm a friend. I'm not your friend,
just thought you had a right to know.

Marriage Guidance

Who wears a cloak of woven gold?
Has no-one told you glam is out,
that foxy royals favour shabby chic?
These days it's all about the bold
rejection of convention, so shout
it from the highest turret; weak
is the woman who marries for wealth—
a rich man would happily marry himself.

Who would wear this feathered cloak?
Do you think the geese would give
the very things that make them free,
without a fight? The kind of bloke
who breaks a wing would have you live
in batteries, clipped and flightless. He
may lure you with his cooing words,
but choosing to be caged is for the birds.

Who would wear this cloak of reeds,
this fragile undergrowth? Dream
if you must of acquiescence in the hush
of consecrated sheets, imagining he'd
kiss you, tug gently at your seams,
then shred your delicacy rush by rush.
But, princess, here's the bitter news;
love is just lust in sensible shoes.

The Cryptographer's Song

It takes time to generate these ciphers;
the symbols on the shopping lists,
the codewords on the national news,
the knowing randomness of crossword clues
in broadsheets, patterns that we know.
We come and go, leave moments
for each other like a dead letter drop.
Lights go on and off and on in morse.

In Nissen huts the women go to work
assimilating data, raking through the numbers,
in search of sequences or correlations,
knowing nothing is as random as it seems,
that tiny revelations are not accidents of sound
or light. In time they may decrypt the words
we are afraid to say: that both of us would
rather die alone before revealing anything.

Sour Jewel

i.m. *Billy MacKenzie*

I think it was the bustle of the place
that did for me, the record shop
oblivious, impersonal, that voice
above the local noise, here a joyful skip

and swoop, there the grating edge of teeth.
Billy's gone I heard. *The stupid sod
has done it.* No doubting such a truth
when all you knew of him said

this was how he'd always meant to go.
Surely he was asking for it, crooning
Gloomy Sunday down at Fat Sam's, grey
clouds round the baby grand, brewing

retribution in the belly of a double bass.
He'd done the city thing, there and back,
and back again. He left behind the house
he'd never known, the loaded deck

that dealt him aces, all of which he'd fold.
Somewhere there must be that feral
out-take from the studio, the wild
and lonely *dies irae* sung as a recessional,

his steep falsetto rise let off the leash,
foreshortened by the accidental melting
of the precious piece of vinyl, out of reach,
a limited edition, perhaps the only pressing.

Lucifer

His children are intentionally blank,
obscure in cave-wall smudges,
indistinct in pointillist pea-soup,
or mile-wide pixellated smiles
on restless city billboards. They are
often blurred in centre ground
behind the despot's level stare,
or whispering into the ready ear
of tyrants. Sometimes they
are there, with hand upon the arm
of those who write the tracts,
or handing round the solid fuel
at martyrings and lynchings. If they pray,
their prayers must be persistence
of the graphic arts, for mass
communication, and for drums.

They haven't written much about me yet
but maybe when I read my press
I'll see the pages scorch and catch.
I dare not wander by your room
in case you hear the thud of hoof
and smell the smoking carpet as I pass.

The Talk Of The North

Its bone-white marquee billed it as
The Talk Of The North, but no-one talks
that way today. Wild nights lit its face
with lamps in crushed velour and lace,
once cream, now kippered brown
by fumes of love, a pheromonal
soup observable from space.

Once, jitterbugging pairs would leap
and circle like the pistons of a train.
Boys perfecting steps with lovebit teens,
till bingo masters called slow death
on Tuesday evening's empty house.
Through brume of smoke, the glitterball
fragmented them to disco smithereens.

Now wreckers turn the brickwork
into broken teeth, while dancers watch.
I saw them all again at dawn, cavorting
naked in what light the sky could spare,
swaying round the blackened henge,
exalting its unlikely calibration
of their weeks and months and years.

Sunburst Finish

For him, just fourteen years, the book came first,
a Christmas gift from quiet Uncle Jack.
Bert Weedon, virtuoso king of strings,
beard-wearer of the year in '56,
grinning from the frontispiece.
Play In A Day? The lying bastard.

His piggy bank grew fat on paper rounds,
until the shop exchanged his gold for wood
and stainless steel, the maple body
glowing on the racking in the darkened store.
Money talks. His said goodbye, but waved
as he departed with the flight case on his back.

The case stood in the shadows in the spare room
every night, as stern as Johnny Cash,
nearly-black with alligator flesh,
silver buckled waist and streaks of sweat,
thick white stitching down each shoulder,
gaunt and watchful as a crow.

He learned some chords, but couldn't play
the tunes his daughter knew, her blood so weak
from isotopes towards the end, the charts
once bright but now so full of junk. The case
had shrunk but still he hoovered round it every week,
a snake-skinned coffin, too small for a man
but large enough to carry children from this world.

Queuing For Water

Soldier says another hour from where we stand
to the spout-end of the line. Jerry cans in hand,

we recall the summer storms that washed us off
the street in seconds, or when reservoirs were rough

with runoff from the moors; now we hope for dregs
or heavy dew. Girl from number nine (bruised legs,

unruly child) is talking to the widow from the flats,
telling her she's short of nothing that she's got.

I recall the water-fights as kids, the cold cling
of sodden shirt, and how you would give anything

to be that wet again; since then I've desiccated
by degrees and taken fewer baths. We've waited

long for signs the empty skies might break
and turn the dustbowl of this town into a lake.

The line moves faster as the standpipe nears,
anticipating every drip. A Corporal appears,

strikes my surname from his dog-eared list,
and says *This is all there is. You have to make it last.*

Painting by Numbers

For J Campbell Kerr

In the loft of the red Lubyanka, at the crown
of the Kingsway, there's a studio, cool and bright,
where the painter sits, stealing the ochre-brown
from blisters of rock in the outback, spiriting white
from the blankness of polar ice and snowmelt rush,
liberating sweltered greens and yellows from the veldt,
forging the blue of fluke and fin, rust of Sahara dusk,
the counterfeited black from notches in Orion's belt.

His loaded brushwork saturates the knock-off scenes
that hail from platform kiosks or from trolleys
wheeled through long-stay wards; the magazines
that call themselves *your friend*. The haggard glory
of the harbourfront at Rothesay or the Moray Firth
are paraphrased in Polynesian hues, poster-bold,
and yet in fugitive colours; a rendering of Earth
no single room or page or name could ever hold.

Rorschach Test

'One half of the world cannot understand the pleasures
of the other'.
                          —Jane Austen, *Emma*

She reads Austen day and night; excited
by the chaste manoeuvring and snobbery
disguised as taste. He rolls his eyes and says
that he can only take so much deliberation;
for God's sake, if you fancy someone, ask.

She watches as he channel-hops, seeing
just a flash of Edward Ferrars, breeches
bulging, shirt unbuttoned down to there,
smouldering with virtue in between his
flares of cruelty and casual machismo.

Upstairs now, she has his full attention.
Her fingers braided in his hair, she
holds him down until he has delighted her
for long enough. Two centuries away
the author spatters ink across a page,

her manuscript a Rorschach Test; look
closely—*what's the first thing that you see?*
A butterfly, embalmed and mounted;
the flayed pelt of some great beast;
two people pulling on a slender rope.

The Vanquished

What is left
are minor unresolved disturbances in equilibrium,
the broken vase that only one of them has cause to mention,
the weight of books they lay aside at dusk.

Cholecystectomy

Somewhere there's an excised part of me,
a mermaid's purse suspended in a jar,
sheathing calculi like musket balls,
trembling in formaldehyde at fall of foot.
I'm told it is redundant, a worm cast of gut
that narrows to a fundus; a small
incision, a porting out of flesh, a scar
or two, and then I can forget its treachery.

This strange birth was painless; just the hiss
of valves, the pre-med gathering dusk
about me, then the darkness like a wall
collapsing. Something in that little death
remained throughout my sleep; a breath
of entonox, and I, slipping down, recall
the surgeon joking through his mask,
saying *what I do not need I will not miss.*

There are other parts that serve
no purpose; bone spurs, polyps, warts,
appendices and other phony organs.
I could fill up jar on jar. And so, the line
that sutures up the days runs out at mine,
leaving just this dynasty of orphans
dormant in their demijohns, their thoughts
lost in the future I neglected to preserve.

Show Me A Man's Teeth

and I will tell you who he is, or what.
Don't give me grey forensic finds
but cultured pearls that grow
around a living tongue. Show me
the tilt of their owner's chin,
the rictus that betrays them
like a kiss, the lantern jaw or overbite
that hints at light in-breeding,
the wax-eyed drunk
with two yellowed rotten rows,
who smokes the guns to sleep.
The nervous girl who rolls up
at the shoot, whose agent paid a grand
to get them fixed, whose make-up girl
sends texts and reassures her
as she rouges up her nipples
that they're looking at her smile—
don't you think her every thought
was known the second
that she opened up to show me
her impossible dentition?

At bloodstock sales and selling plates,
one glance into the ring of white
inside the noble mouth
can mark a beast as thoroughbred
or meat. So it is with me.
Fillings are a giveaway,
but gaps between are secrets
held in sleep; the sliding tackle,
the playtime scrap you couldn't hope

to win, the blood, your mother saying
nice boys don't get into fights,
the space she used to occupy,
the bridge from milk to wisdom.

The Unification Church Of Dr Robert Moog

'The illusion of choice is an indication of a lack of freedom.'
—Ken MacLeod

You've drunk denominations,
like a thirsty man who works his way
along the single malts behind the bar.
You've conformed and nonconformed,
lurched from Trappist isolation
to unhappy clapper, heard a priest
weep through a grille and wondered
who was whose confessor.

You've laid your hands on the radio,
waiting for the ministry that heals
but found neither God nor Devil
in the fug of backmasked voices.
But if there's room in your soul
for one more schism, step this way;
The Church of Christ, Synthesist,
welcomes you and all your noise,

saying *life is the great sine wave;*
peak follows trough follows peak.
You cannot shape its form, just
its frequency; amplify or diminish
it if you will. There can be no peace
for us, fettered as we are by choice,
but here's our mantra of the week;
Attack. Sustain. Decay. Release.

Ten Gigs I Never Went To

Let us assume a curvature of space,
that time can be folded like paper.
If this were so I could laze and sip coffee
in the now, then walk the shortest route
between two points, over to myself
at eighteen, standing in the rain
outside the Manchester Apollo, half of
Northern England in the queue ahead,
waiting for the opening of the doors.

Those who know the science of this
gravitate by subterfuge to call boxes,
dialling themselves across the years.
The phone booths that ring and ring
when no-one's there to answer:
that's them, attempting to connect to us
before the splinter-moment that the girl
that got away walks by, or seconds
from the worst decision of our lives.

If I could, I'd tap me on the shoulder,
have a word; *get out of here*. Across
the city there's a secret gig, a carefree act
about to change the world. Trust me,
some day you'll wish that you had gone.

The Naming of Hurricanes

Sometimes in summertime a hangdog
weather man stands in front of shots

panning over Caribbean villas mangled
into matchwood, corpses of beached yachts,

palms ripped from sand. A time-lapsed arc
maps the march of this year's cyclone,

wheeling to make its landfall, jerk
the world around it. Last year's was *Joan*,

a hurricane with personality—in yer face,
busy, our eyes drawn to her in photographs

as she breezed in and out, visible from space,
leaving nothing standing in her path.

I wonder who compiles the list of names;
whose mother, daughter, lover, wife

brings to mind such desolation. The Janes
and Brendas all suggest ordinary life

might yet return once the summer storm
has blown itself into a half-remembered breeze.

Here, so far from paradise, the house is warm,
but colder winds are forecast from the east,

and suddenly the sky is full of clouds. A chill
simmers round my feet, and I think it's best

we do not name this storm. Already it has filled
the room, blown your final letter off my desk.

An Assumption Of Monsters

He told her there was something underneath her bed,
a fiend in slumber or a golem made from dust.
He promised to protect her, with no thought beyond
the flowers and the vows. She coupled with his ghost,
cooked dinners for the shape of what he'd been.
She loved a slasher film but sat and cursed
through all his arty flicks. She smoothed the bristles
of his fur, imagined poison pumping through his chest,
and wondered if his coat concealed the bludgeon
which would one day beat her skull until it burst.

She recognised the tightening of his jaw, the subtle
clicks and tics below his voice, the way he pursed
his lips before a kiss, as if the act of mingling their spittle
could pass her sickness on to him. This was not the worst
—his tongue would burn his symbol on the mantle
of her flesh, and she would squirm and twist,
denying him again. It wasn't always possible
to tell the demons from the humans they possessed,
or to look the monster in the eye until the final
frenzied reel, with its unmasking of the beast.

I Am The Man Who Winds The Doomsday Clock

sure that you, like me, lament the lack
of tension which necessitates its winding.
The fading of the hour, when bloc bloc bloc
was how you marked your understanding
of yourselves, has seen you shoring up the weak,
ingesting their slow poisons. Now you're finding
middle ways to keep them from the shock
of rumbling battalions descending
on their undetermined borders. You make pacts
encompassing the merest ones of them, befriending
even those whose full-fat ideologies you reject.

Surely you must long for generals in spider-black,
fronting up their juntas, unearned medals jostling
for room with golden frogging, launch code books
a hand's reach away? Did you ever see them selling
off their sovereignty vows for piles of stock,
or ceding land for shares in offshore drilling?
Thank God the planet's dying, then, Geiger clicks
fading, and yet you always have the means of killing
what you cannot understand, going back
to what you call your nature. Blue chip stocks are falling
as I wind the minute hand around to twelve o'clock,
till all is silence in the gap between the tick and tock.

The Mockers

It could be that you didn't cross your fingers,
or perhaps you missed that hopeful puff
into your palm before you cast the dice,

or maybe you neglected to salute the lonely
magpie sentry on the bypass. Maybe
something in your prayer wasn't right,

a presumption your petition would be heard.
Perhaps you should have worn the lucky
shirt again. It worked last time, your team

three up in half an hour. Remember when
you failed to take the normal route to work,
took the rat-run past the Cats Protection League,

Sandy Denny turned up loud? The soot-black tom
that ran across the road outside, that jelly-thud
below your smoking tyres. The time you missed

the space above your shoulder, scattered salt
all down your suit? You laughed so hard
it turned the milk. That time the brolly opened

by itself, your windmill flailing, trying to contain
the blossoming eclipse before it fell across
you, eating up your shadow. That bloody

owl in the early afternoon, his *whit-to-whoos,*
eleven, twelve, thirteen. The surgeon with your file
who does not frown but does not smile,

who takes his shoes off, puts them on the table.
The sweating horse that shelters in the field—
what does it suspect, indeed, what does it know?

The Tenth Muse

Does it matter what it was
that brought him to the boil
like that? I heard a knuckle crack,
felt the quiet room recoil

watched him as he calmly tugged
the ripcord of his mouth, letting out
those trammelled imprecations.
At no point did he shout

but rather let the swearing do
its grisly work. I didn't know
what half his curses meant,
inventive portmanteaux

and reference to body parts
I'd never seen, each new profanity
a drawing back of shutters
on a charnel house, till all could see

the pulsing foulness. I admired,
despite myself, his slashing fluency,
wondered if he'd worked for years
to purify his caustic obloquy,

preparing for the moment when
object and subject coalesced.
They say a spectre comes to them at night,
carving wild inventions on their breast,

Malakas, the outcast Muse,
floating like a grawlix in the space
above their head, seducing then
polluting them with noxious grace.

My own minced oaths are signs
that I exist within myself, my neck
wound in, condemned eternally
to burn, alone, in the flames of heck.

Grawlix: A string of typographical symbols, used (especially
in comic strips) to represent an obscenity or swearword.

Three Elegies for Minor Shakespearean Characters

Fleance

Our speculative histories ascribe to you
paternity of houses, positing inheritances
we may never know. The dad that left
you for dead now hams it up in shadows

and shakes his gory locks at rubberneckers,
but you were never crushed by a soliloquy
or struck down by the seizures of the plot;
indeed, your surest act was to fly, fly, fly.

Fortinbras

Life's a bag of mouldy fruit, my friend,
and history is shoulder-deep in scum
who never got what should have come
to them, ended up at the blunt end

of the dagger. We all feel the blood
stir for what is lost, but life's seldom fair
and some of you are really only there
to make the rest of us look good.

Mercutio

The gang refuse to talk or drink with you
for fear that you might sit them down
and tell them straight; how passion's just
the *antipasto* to the *primo piatto* of regret.

You may laugh at all the Romeos you've met,
yet still respect their Juliets (as all men must)
but, because there is a Tybalt in every town,
un uomo has to do what *un uomo* has to do.

Trace Elements

—*Popular Science,* June 1926

There's water in me, buckets of the stuff,
but not the spell to turn it into wine.

Despite the fat for seven bars of soap,
my hands in these intrigues are seldom clean.

There's lime to whitewash half a wall,
yet all those shades in me that have no name.

Sugar too, to sweeten just one drink,
stirred into tasteless crushes once again.

Sufficient iron here to cast a coffin nail,
a forging of myself in brittle steel.

A tiny cache of sulphur, just enough to purge
a dog of fleas, and yet the itch is in me still.

Bromine in a shot glass, downed in one to dull
that urge, yet there it is, in every swishing hem.

A pinch of arsenic, although too small
to lay me out. There just as a warning then?

And lithium—there should be just a dash,
a measured dose to keep my tethered poles apart.

Phosphorus to fuel a match or two,
but nothing rough to strike a lasting spark.

Mine is an equilibrium that regulates
itself. The rising moon. The setting sun.

The whole sustains by balancing the parts.
The good. The bad. The all. The one.

Love Song of the Bodysnatcher

Come with me, through the stark years.
Together we will ride the glacier,
watch the television with no sound,
take photos with an empty camera,
light cigarettes but not smoke, pour beer
into glasses made from air, hang around.

I'll show you how to find your truest self
in sleep, share contra-indications of love
with you, the pang that's just a side-effect
of chemical imbalances, a rough
copy of a rough copy birthed in stealth.
We adapt and we survive. *You're next.*

Vanishing Point

Here is rest, your journey's end. The welcome mat
put out for you says *this is now the place where you belong.*

Here is food, and drink. We're guessing that
you haven't had a meal in days. Eat up, grow strong.

Here is work, to liberate yourself. No time for chat.
The music of your industry will be a selfless song.

Here is order. Nothing's overlooked. Your hat
and coat please. Only we decide if this is wrong.

Wilkommen. Witajcie. Dobro pozhalovat.
Stay in line. No talking there. Now, move along.

Acknowledgments

Acknowledgments are due to the editors of the following publications in which some of these poems first appeared:

Advice on Proposals (edited by Angela Topping, Like This Press, 2014), *Blackbox Manifold, By Grand Central Station We Sat Down And Wept* (Edited by Kevin Cadwallender, Red Squirrel Press, 2010), *Drey, Drifting Down The Lane* (edited by Harriette Lawler and Agnes Marton, 2013), *Dundee Writes, The Flight of the Turtle: New Writing Scotland 29* (edited by Alan Bissett & Carl MacDougall, ASLS, 2011), *Gutter, Ink, Sweat and Tears, Magma, New Writing Dundee, Newspaper Taxis* (edited by Phil Bowen, Damian Furniss & David Woolley, Seren Press 2013), *Not Only The Dark* (edited by Jo Field and Nicky Gould, Categorical Books, 2011), *Rising, The Robin Hood Book* (edited by Alan Morrison & Angela Topping, Caparison Press, 2013), *Royal Wedding Poems* (Poemcatcher, 2011), *Sweet Breast and Acid Tongue* (edited by Angela Topping, Like This Press, 2014), *Trespass* and *Where Rockets Burn Through* (edited by Russell Jones, Penned In The Margins, 2012).

'Allogeneic' was Runner-Up in the Hippocrates Prize in 2012. 'Fàgail' was Runner-Up in the Baker Prize in 2013. 'Girl From The Polders' was a Runner-Up in the National Galleries of Scotland 'Inspired' competition in 2011.